Just Breathe!

Inspirational Quotes
For Caregivers

Compiled by BJ Smith

Dedicated to my mother, whose unconditional love, laughter, and courage will always inspire me in life. I love you, Mom.

Katherine Calhoun

1928-2011

Breathe: to be alive; live, to pause
to rest or regain breath

Breathe easily/easy/freely: to be
relaxed or relieved, especially after a
period of tension

Introduction

Breathing seemed to be the most difficult act for me to do as I cared for my mother, who for seven years suffered from Alzheimer's disease. She was the most beautiful woman, both inside as well as out. Wise and spirited are great words to describe her. She fought for a life and family she loved and cherished just to watch it slip away, day by day, into a dark abyss. The day my mother and I went to the neurologist I had a feeling of what the doctor would tell us. When the actual words *Alzheimer's disease* were spoken, I felt as if I had just been kicked in the gut. I couldn't breathe! I tried so hard not to look scared and broken in front of my mom. All I could hear was my mother ask, "What does Alzheimer's mean and how is it going to affect me?"

From that day began a seven-year adventure full of every emotion the human body can experience. Together as a team, we agreed to make the best of the inevitable. I learned to live in the Alzheimer's world with her and then fall apart to my husband and family at home. Trying to be the perfect daughter, mother, wife, and sole caregiver became unmanageable.

To be all of this is impossible and guilt began overwhelming me daily.

As a caregiver, watching a loved one disappear before your eyes begins to whittle away at your emotional and mental state. Then the day comes when you feel like you can't breathe and you're being suffocated. The brightness of your own life is darkening. You ask yourself, "Where have I gone?" As a caregiver you lose a part of yourself when taking care of a loved one but if you look at your world a little differently you will see that what you have gained on your journey is astounding.

Among the negatives, there were also positives gained during my experience with my mother and her horrible disease. As I tried to cope inside her Alzheimer's world, I learned to stay calm during any crises because this made her world stress-free. She saw life as if through the eyes of a child. The colors around her were brighter and bolder. Sounds were crisper and clearer. Everyone was her friend and she didn't experience sadness. WOW! It doesn't get better than that.

When we began to balance out our days and I finally asked for the help that I desperately needed, a bond developed between my mother and me that was a precious surprise. We always had a wonderful relationship but the deep and strong bond that began to develop was one that only another caregiver would be able to understand. I began to feel blessed that I was the one that was able to help her and guide her through such a difficult part of her life. Whenever she had a moment of clarity and grew agitated at her situation, I would share my secret with her to say, "Just breathe!" We would take a few deep breaths and I would begin telling her a story about my children that she had heard at least twenty times. She enjoyed it as if it was the first. We began to laugh more than we cried.

The pages that follow are not only for caregivers to Alzheimer's patients but for all caregivers who need a moment of inspiration in their crazy world. The quotes included are ones that daily motivated and inspired me. There are new ones that I wish I had been aware of for those really difficult days. I have always kept a ceramic dry-erase board in my kitchen with a daily quote that pertained to my day or week. They are great reminders that I can get through anything God hands me. That board still has quotes on it that are positive and uplifting to help my family and I through our day.

My healing after the loss of my mother is progressing, as will yours—but until then, remember to "Just breathe!"

BJ Smith

Focusing on the act of breathing clears the mind of all daily distractions and clears our energy, enabling us to better connect with the Spirit within.

-Unknown

Learn how to exhale, the inhale will take care of itself.

-Carla Melucci Ardito

No act of kindness, no matter how small, is ever wasted.

-Aesop

Laughter and tears are both responses to frustration and exhaustion. I myself prefer to laugh, since there is less cleaning up to do afterwards.

-Kurt Vonnegut

Strength means recognizing that it is impossible to be strong all of the time.

-Sally Franser

The healthy and strong individual is the one who asks for help when he needs it.

-Rona Barrett

Don't be sad; don't be angry if life deceives you! Submit to your grief; your time for joy will come, believe me.

-Aleksandr Pushkin

Nothing is worth more than this day.

-Goethe

To the world you are someone, but to someone you are the world.

-Unknown

Sometimes it helps to know that I just can't do it all. One step at a time is all that's possible—even when those steps are taken on the run.

-Anne W. Schaef

Do not let what you cannot do interfere with what you can do.

-John Woodson

The measure of love is to love without measure.

-Saint Augustine

Through humor, you can soften some of the worst blows that life delivers. And once you find laughter, no matter how painful your situation might be, you can survive it.

-Bill Cosby

The secret of many a man's success in the world resides in his insight into the moods of men and his tact in dealing with them.

-J.G. Holland

Courage is not the absence of fear, but rather the willingness to act in spite of it.

-Unknown

Kind words are the music of the world.

-F.W. Faber

Never part without loving words to think of during your absence. It may be that you will not meet gain in this life.

-Jean Paul Richter

Words have wings...so
Speak good things.

Anon

Character is doing the right thing
when nobody is looking.

-FJ.C. Watts

Too often we underestimate the power of touch, a smile, a kind word, a listening ear, an honest compliment, or the smallest act of caring, all of which have the potential to turn a life around.

-Leo Buscaglia

Look to be treated by others as you have treated others.

-Publius Syrus

Never lose a chance of saying a kind word.

-William Thackeray

The most important things in the world have been accomplished by people who have kept trying when there seemed to be no hope at all.

-Dale Carnegie

You must look into other people as well as at them.

-Lord Chesterfield

The first duty of love is to listen.

-Paul Tillich

Nothing in life is to be feared, it is only to be understood. Now is the time to understand more, so that we may fear less.

-Marie Curie

Patience is the best remedy for every trouble.

-Titus Maccius Plautus

It's not the load that breaks you down, it's the way you carry it.

-Lena Horne

A difficult time can be more readily endured if we retain the conviction that our existence holds a purpose, a cause to pursue, a person to love, a goal to achieve.

-John Maxwell

The fragrance of what you give stays with you.

-Earl Allen

Love means to love that which is unlovable. Otherwise it is no virtue at all.

-G.K. Chesterton

In helping others, we shall help ourselves, for whatever good we give out
completes the circle and comes back
to us.

-Flora Edwards

23

One person caring about another rep-
resents life's greatest value.

-Jim Rohn

If you can't change your fate, change
your attitude.

-Amy Tan

I have the choice of being constantly active and happy or introspectively passive and sad, or I can go mad by ricocheting in between.

-Silvia Plath

The miracle is this—the more we share, the more we have.

-Leonard Nimoy

If you see someone without a smile... give them one of yours!

-Unknown

Remember always that you not only have the right to be an individual, you have an obligation to be one.

-Eleanor Roosevelt

Impossible situations can become possible miracles.

-Robert H. Schuller

Be determined to handle any challenge in a way that will make you grow.

-Les Brown

Breathe. Let go. And remind yourself that this very moment is the only one you know you have for sure.

-Oprah Winfrey

Things turn out best for those who make the best of the way things turn out.

-Jack Buck

There is no failure except in no longer trying.

-Elbert Hubbard

It is not what we get. But who we become, what we contribute...that gives meaning to our lives.

—Anthony Robbins

Remember sadness is always temporary. This, too, shall pass.

-Chuck T. Falcon

Self-sacrifice is the real miracle out of which all the reported miracles grow.

-Ralph Waldo Emerson

Be willing to have it so. Acceptance of what has happened is the first step to overcoming the consequences of any misfortune.

-William James

The best way to find yourself, is to lose yourself in the service of others.

-Ghandi

Learn to love, now.

-Brandon Boyd

It's your unlimited power to care and to love that can make the biggest difference in the quality of someone's life.

-Unknown

Reach Out. Share.
Smile. Hug.

-Og Mandino

God gave burdens, he also gave shoul-
ders.

-Yiddish Proverbs

God will not permit any troubles to come upon us, unless He has a specific plan by which great blessing can come out of the difficulty.

-Peter Marshall

An inconvenience is an adventure wrongly considered.

-G.K. Chesterton

Love is the great miracle cure. Loving ourselves works miracles in our lives.

-Louise Hay

One of the most valuable things we can do to heal one another is listen to each other's stories.

-Rebecca

Each difficult moment has the potential to open my eyes and my heart.

-Myla Kabat-Zinn

Find little ways to make a part of your day like a day off.

-Unknown

The best and most beautiful things in the world cannot be seen or even touched-they must be felt with the heart.

-Helen Keller

Bear the inevitable with dignity.

-Streckfuss

Every problem has a gift for you in its hands.

-Richard Bach

Happiness is an attitude. We either make ourselves miserable, or happy and strong. The amount of work is the same.

-Francesca Reigler

The most wasted of all days is one without laughter.

-E.E. Cummings

Forgiveness is not an occasional act: it is an attitude.

-Martin Luther King Jr.

The beginning of anxiety is the end of faith, and the beginning of true faith is the end of anxiety.

-George E. Mueller

There is no exercise better for the heart than reaching down and lifting people up.

-John Andrews Holmes Jr

Determination that just won't quit— that's what it takes.

-A.J. Foyt

Have patience with all things, but chiefly have patience with yourself. Do not lose courage in considering your own imperfections, but instantly set about remedying them—every day begin the task anew.

-St. Francis de Sales

Real difficulties can be overcome; it's the imaginary ones that are unconquerable.

-Theodore N. Vail

What can't be cured, must be endured.

-Old Saying

A positive attitude may not solve all your problems, but it will annoy enough people to make it worth the effort.

-Herm Albright

Crisis refines life. In them you discover who you are.

-Allan K. Chalmers

When you feel like falling down, don't
give up.

-Samantha Smile

Don't let your mind bully your body into believing it must carry the burden of its worries.

—Astrid Alauda

The purpose of man is to live, not to exist.

-Jack London

Life is either a daring adventure or nothing.

-Helen Keller

Goodness in words creates trust, goodness in thinking creates depth, goodness in giving creates love.

-Lao Tse

You must do the things you think you cannot do.

-Eleanor Roosevelt

Lord, grant that I might not so much seek to be loved as to love.

-St. Francis of Assisi

You cannot tailor make your situation on life, but you can tailor make the attitudes to fit those situations.

-Zig Ziglar

Nothing can bring you peace but yourself.

-Ralph Waldo Emerson

The greatest weapon against stress is our ability to choose one thought over another.

-William James

A good deed is never lost: he who sows courtesy reaps friendship; and he who plants kindness gathers love.

-Basil

Be good to yourself 'cause nobody else has the power to make you happy.

-George Michael

Life shrinks or expands in proportion to one's courage.

-Anaïs Nin

Most of the shadows of this life are caused by our standing in our own sunshine.

-Ralph Waldo Emerson

59

Loving is the most unmitigated and cou-
rageous act I perform in a day.

-Mary Anne Radmacher

I'm not afraid of storms for I'm learning
to sail my ship.

-Louisa May Alcott

Self-pity is our worst enemy and if we yield to it, we can never do anything wise in this world.

-Helen Keller

What happens to a person is less sig-
nificant than what happens within him.

-Louis L. Mann

The soul of conversation is sympathy.

-Thomas Campbell

Feelings come and go like clouds in the sky. Conscious breathing is my anchor.

-Thich Nhat Hanh

Doing good to others is not a duty, it is a joy, for it increases our health and happiness.

-Zoroaster

Let me not pray to be sheltered from dangers, but to be fearless in facing them.

-Rabindranath Tagore

You set yourself up for happiness or you set yourself up for sadness. Either way, it's your doing.

-Jill Davis

Laughter is the sun that drives winter from the human face.

-Victor Hugo

Compassion is a verb.

-Thich Nhat Hanh

I'm going to get through this; I'm going to be fine. The power to do it is all in my mind.

-Cindy Wagner

In doing something, do it with love or never do it at all.

-Ghandi

Either you run the day or the day runs you.

-Jim Rohn

Your best is going to change from moment to moment; it will be different when you are healthy as opposed to sick. Under any circumstances, simply do your best, and you will avoid self-judgment, self-abuse and regret.

-Miguel Ruiz

Nothing is impossible, the word itself says "I'm possible!"

-Audrey Hepburn

He that can have patience, can have what he will.

-Benjamin Franklin

*A man can do only what a man can do.
But if he does that each day he can
sleep at night and do it again the next
day.*

—Albert Schweitzer

Our own life has to be our message.

-Thich Nhat Hanh

You, as much as anyone in the universe, deserve your love and respect.

-Buddha

Find the courage to ask questions and to express what you really want. Communicate with others as clearly as you can to avoid misunderstandings, sadness and drama. With just this one agreement, you can completely transform your life.

-Miguel Ruiz

They invented hugs to let people know you love them without saying anything.

-Bill Keane

The most beautiful gift we can give each other is the truth.

-Unknown

I have the right to seek help from others even though my loved one may object. I recognize the limits of my own endurance and strength.

-Jo Horne

Problems are not stop signs, they are guidelines.

-Robert H. Schuller

What you do today can improve all your tomorrows.

-Ralph Marston

When another person makes you suffer, it is because he suffers deeply within himself, and his suffering is spilling over. He does not need punishment; he needs help.

That's the message he is sending.

-Thich Nhat Hanh

Wherever you are—be all there.

-Jim Elliot

We make the world we live in shape our own environment.

-Orison Swett Marden

Hope is important because it can make the present moment less difficult to bear. If we believe that tomorrow will be better, we can bear a hardship today.

-Thich Nhat Hanh

The way to cheer yourself up is to cheer everyone else up.

-Mark Twain

One of the secrets of life is to make stepping stones out of stumbling blocks.

-Jack Penn

Nothing others do is because of you. What others say and do is a projection of their own reality, their own dream. When you are immune to the opinions and actions of others, you won't be the victim of needless suffering.

-Miguel Ruiz

What comes from the heart, goes to the heart.

-Samuel Taylor Coleridge

All problems become smaller if you don't dodge them but confront them.

-William F. Halsey

I have a right to take pride in what I am accomplishing and to applaud the courage it sometimes takes to meet the needs of my loved one.

-Jo Horne

I promise myself that I will enjoy every minute of the day that is given to me to live.

-Thich Nhat Hanh

Our sorrows and wounds are healed only when we touch them with compassion.

-Buddha

There is only one way...to get any-body to do anything. And that is by making the other person want to do it.

-Dale Carnegie

Strength does not come from physical capacity. It comes from an indomitable will.

-Ghandi

The greatest revenge is to accomplish what others say you cannot do.

-Unknown

Patience can't be acquired overnight. It is just like building a muscle, every day you need to work on it.

-Eknath Easwaran

Kind words can be short and easy to speak, but their echoes are truly endless.

-Mother Theresa

When you reach the end of your rope, tie a knot in it and hang on.

-Thomas Jefferson

We come to love not by finding a perfect person, but by learning to see an imperfect person perfectly.

-Sam Keen

Life's challenges are not supposed to paralyze you, they're supposed to help you discover who you are.

-Bernice Johnson Reagon

I have a right to get angry, depressed and express other difficult emotions occasionally.

-Jo Horne

Waking up this morning, I smile. Twenty-four brand new hours are before me. I vow to live fully in each moment and to look at all beings with eyes of compassion.

-Thich Nhat Hanh

As one person I cannot change the world, but I can change the world of one person.

-Paul Shane Spear

You give but little when you give of your possession. It is when you give of yourself that you truly give

-K. Gibran

Love is the productive form of related-
ness to other and to oneself. It implies
responsibility, care, and knowledge,
and the width for the other person
to grow and develop. It is expression
of intimacy between two human beings
under the conditions of the preserva-
tion of each other's integrity.

-Eric Fromm

Some people care too much, I think it's called love.

-Winnie the Pooh

If you can laugh at it, you can live with it.

-Unknown

A sense of humor can help you over-look the unattractive, tolerate the unpleasant, cope with the unexpected, and smile through the unbearable.

-Moshe Waldocks

95

A single sunbeam can drive away many shadows.

-St Francis of Assisi

People are often unreasonable, illogical, and self-centered; forgive them anyway. If you are kind, people may accuse you of selfish, ulterior motives; be kind anyway. If you are honest and frank, people may cheat you; be honest and frank anyway. You see, the final analysis, it is between you and God; it was never between you and them anyway.

-Mother Teresa

There is no medicine like hope, no incentive so great, and no tonics so powerful as expectation of something better tomorrow.

-O Swett Marden

Stress is not what happens to us. It's our response to what happens. And response is something we can choose.

-Maureen Killoran

I've learned that people will forget what you said, people will forget what you did, but they will never forget how you made them feel.

-Maya Angelou

Be a rainbow in someone else's cloud.

-Maya Angelou

A loving heart is the truest wisdom.

-Charles Dickens

Hope begins in the dark, the stubborn hope that if you just show up and try to do the right thing, the dawn will come. You wait and watch and work; you don't give up.

—Anne Lamott

CPSIA information can be obtained at www.ICGtesting.com
Printed in the USA
BVOW03s1529131014

370608BV00010B/130/P